"the nailhead that held the South's two

VICKSBURG

A PHOTOGRAPHIC JOURNEY
WITH VOICES FROM THE PAST

PHOTOGRAPHS BY HELEN S. SCHWARTZ
TEXT BY KATHARINE A. SLOAN
EDITED BY KRISTIN D. MURRAY

Published by Artistry in Photography
P.O. Box 491 Langhorne, PA 19047

Front cover quote:
President Jefferson Davis
Quoted in: Vicksburg: Fall of the Confederate Gibraltar, edited by Terrence J. Winschel p. 14

Back cover quote:
President Abraham Lincoln
Quoted in: Vicksburg, by William C. Everhart
published National Park Service, Washington, DC, 1954, pg 53

Front cover photos: Memorial Arch at Vicksburg NMP, Old Courthouse Museum, and looking at the Great Redoubt from Battery De Goyler

Back cover photo and page 7: Mississippi River

Page 112: Mississippi State Flower, Magnolia, photographed in the National Cemetery in Vicksburg NMP

Cover/inside designs: Helen Schwartz and Gail Kehler   Desktop layout and design: Helen Schwartz and Alex Mac Donald

All production and packaging: Helen S. Schwartz

ISBN # 978-0-9776959-5-9

Other books published by Artistry in Photography: "Tell Them All About It, Won't You?" Images of the Present, Voices of the Past Gettysburg ISBN# 0-9776959-1-3

Published by Artistry in Photography
Artistry Publications, Inc.
P.O. Box 491 Langhorne, PA 19047
e-mail- info@ArtistryInPhotography.com
web site- www.artistryinphotography.com

MADE AND PRINTED IN THE UNITED STATES OF AMERICA

For Albert & Michael
Our brothers of the heart who are sorely missed

Acknowledgments

With gratitude and respect, we acknowledge the contributions of the men and women, soldiers, sailors, and civilians, Union and Confederate who struggled and suffered through the siege of Vicksburg .

To all the people we met in Vicksburg, MS who have been so hospitable and helpful; Thank You!   Thanks to those who were involved in reviewing this book, and the Park Rangers for their valuable input. Special thanks to Shanna Farmer for her time, support, and guidance, and to Park Ranger Robbie Smith whose tour brought the siege of Vicksburg to life for us, and for writing the Forward in this book.

Heartfelt gratitude to Mr. Edwin C. Bearss, Chief Historian Emeritus, National Park Service for sharing his direction, encouragement, and support for this book.

Helen S. Schwartz

FORWARD

Vicksburg: A Photographic Journey provides readers with a fresh perspective of one of the most decisive Union victories of the Civil War. High quality and aesthetically pleasing photographs of todays battlefield sites are joined with the eye-witness accounts of participants who experienced different aspects of the Vicksburg campaign. These along with brief explanatory text combine to present a unique vision of Civil War history that transcends time and space. Striking photographs of the battlefield today have the effect of drawing audiences far removed in distance to those sites. Similarly, the accounts of those who experienced first hand the destruction and consequent trauma taking place on the grounds during the Vicksburg campaign allows readers to transcend time to better understand the trials suffered by those north and south during the siege. Finally the descriptive text ties the sites of today with the events of yesterday to give the reader a more full appreciation of hallowed ground and the importance of commemoration. *Vicksburg: A Photographic Journey* gives well deserved attention to an under emphasized site among Civil War battlefields while at the same time illustrates the need of preservation.

Consequently, *Vicksburg: A Photographic Journey* is recommended for anyone who has an interest in Civil War history and preservation. In addition, the nature and quality of the work will likely widen its appeal to include a much more general audience. This in turn will have the promising effect of drawing new Civil War enthusiasts and future preservationists to the cause of ensuring our history is safeguarded for posterity. *Vicksburg: A Photographic Journey* is sure to introduce readers far removed in time and place from the Civil War to the events and actions of the campaign and siege of 145 years ago. Photographer Helen S. Schwartz and writer Katharine A. Sloan are to be commended in their efforts to present a storied battlefield from a new perspective.

Robbie C. Smith
Interpretive Ranger
Vicksburg National Military Park

February 2008

Introduction

"The general impression is that they fire at this city, in that way thinking that they will wear out the women and children and the sick…but they little know the spirit of the Vicksburg women and children if they expect this."

Emma Balfour
Vicksburg Civilian
Quoted in Vicksburg, A City Under Siege: The Diary of Emma Balfour, May 16, 1863 - June 2,1863

In the spring of 2006, the three of us stood overlooking the Mississippi River, a Confederate cannon beside us, a riverboat casino below us, and we tried to imagine what life must have been like in 1863 when the river ran beside the city, controlling its life and fate. Vicksburg is a very different city today than it was during the siege, but there are echoes of those sweltering days in 1863 when death rained from the skies and its civilians burrowed themselves in caves for protection. We walked past the Old Courthouse, now a museum, still flying the Rebel flag, victorious Yankees be damned. Not far away is Pemberton's headquarters, and there we felt the despair as the defender of Vicksburg realized he had to surrender his city and his career.

But it is in the National Park that the voice of the past is the loudest. Driving under the Memorial Arch, we entered the heart of the battle and the siege. We met the ghosts of those who struggled to take the city and those who fought bravely to defend it. Here we could see with our eyes the weather-beaten remains of redans & redoubts, the magnificent hulk of the ironclad Cairo, but it was with our hearts that we heard the stories. We learned of the defiant Mrs. Shirley, refusing to allow her house to be burned. We walked the walls of the Third Louisiana Redan, reeling at the thought of the exploding mine, shuddering at the inner vision of the aftermath. Turning around, we envisioned Coonskin's Tower and atop it, General Grant, peering out at the Confederate lines. Looking up at the gaping hole in the side of the USS Cairo, brought back up from its watery grave, we wondered that not a man was lost.

It was we who were lost, lost in the aching tragedy and beauty of those sultry, deadly 47 days in 1863. Vicksburg has many, many stories to tell.   Are you listening?

Helen S. Schwartz • Katharine A. Sloan • Gail Kehler •
December, 2007

Memorial Arch

"See what a lot of land these fellows hold, of which Vicksburg is the key…Let us get Vicksburg and all that country is ours. The war can never be brought to a close until that key is in our pocket."

Abraham Lincoln, USA
President, United States of America
Quoted in Vicksburg is the Key: The Struggle for the Mississippi River by William L. Shea & Terrence J. Winschel, frontspiece

The imposing Memorial Arch stands at the entrance to Vicksburg National Military Park, inviting you to explore the siege lines of both the Confederate and the Union armies. Built with the remaining funds from the 1917 Blue-Gray Reunion, known as the National Memorial Celebration and Peace Jubilee, held at Vicksburg, the arch was dedicated in 1920.

Minnesota Memorial

"The loss of the enemy…was enormous. The ground in our front and along the road, and either side of the road for several hundred yards way to the right, was thickly strewn with their dead. In numbers of instances two and three dead bodies were piled on each other. Along the road for more than 200 yards the bodies lay so thick that one might have walked the whole distance on them without touching the ground."

Colonel Ashbel Smith, CSA
2^d Texas Infantry
Quoted in Guide to the Vicksburg Campaign edited by Leonard Fullenkamp, Stephen Bowman & Jay Luvaas, p. 403

The 90-foot Minnesota Memorial was dedicated in 1907. At the base of the monument is the figure of a woman representing peace, who sits holding a shield and a sword. The men of the North and South have relinquished their arms and given them to her for safe-keeping. At the base are bronze tablets listing the Minnesota units serving in the Vicksburg Campaign.

11

Michigan Memorial

"A strange stillness pervades our hitherto noisy and tumultuous camp. The men are scattered in every direction, lounging listlessly in the shade, not caring even to play cards, so oppressive is the heat. I am sitting in the shade of a mulberry tree…we alternately write or lounge as the mood takes us. Most assuredly I never felt the heat in Michigan as I feel it here."

Private David Lane, USA
17th Michigan Volunteers
Quoted in Vicksburg: 47 Days of Siege by A.A. Hoehling, p. 190

The spirit of Michigan looks sadly over the ground where her sons fought and died. The statue herself, as well as the lower third of the monument, was carved from one forty ton piece of granite. The 17th Michigan volunteers were part of Welsh's First Division of Major General John G. Parke's 9th Army Corps.   Because the Michiganders were assigned to the Army of the Tennessee in mid-June 1863, they did not participate in the initial assaults against the Vicksburg defenses.

Battery De Golyer

"The batteries opened fire, and soon thereafter the rebel artillery in their works modified and materially slackened fire. About two hours afterward, having previously reconnoitered the ground and received Major-General Logan's assent, I directed Captain DeGolyer's two howitzers to advance about 1,800 yards to the line subsequently occupied by all the light batteries. Fire was immediately opened with good effect, vigorously though not very effectively replied to by the rebel artillery for a short space of time."

Major Charles J. Stolbrand, USA
2[d] Illinois Light Artillery
Quoted in Guide to the Vicksburg Campaign edited by Leonard Fullenkamp, Stephen Bowman & Jay Luvaas, p. 421

Battery De Golyer was named for Captain Samuel De Golyer whose Eighth Michigan Light Artillery was originally positioned here, firing upon the Great Redoubt. A total of twenty-two guns were sent up, making it the largest concentration of Union cannon on the siege line. Earthworks were built up in front of the guns to protect the gunners who were being picked off by Confederate sharpshooters. Unfortunately, they were built too late for Captain De Golyer who was mortally wounded while directing the firing of his guns.

Logan Monument

"Go down to Logan and tell him he is making history today."

Major General Ulysses S. Grant, USA
Commander, United States Army of the Tennessee
Quoted in Vicksburg is the Key: The Struggle for the Mississippi River by William L. Shea & Terrence J. Winschel, p.135

John A. Logan was born in Illinois in 1826. He was another of the "political generals," never having gone to West Point. Logan was elected to the House of Representatives in 1858. He volunteered for the Mexican War in 1846 but saw no combat. He began his military career in earnest as a civilian, fighting alongside the troops at the First Battle of Bull Run while still a member of Congress. Logan raised a regiment and became its colonel, fought at Belmont and was wounded at Fort Donelson. In March 1862, he was promoted to brigadier general and finally resigned his seat in Congress. He commanded the Third Division in McPherson's 17th Army Corps during the Vicksburg Campaign. Promoted to command of the 15th Corps during the Atlanta Campaign in 1864, General Logan assumed command of the Army of the Tennessee upon McPherson's death at the Battle of Atlanta. Despite his proven ability as a commander, Logan was passed over for permanent command of the Army of the Tennessee. Embittered, but still devoted to the Union, he served with distinction as corps commander until the end of the war, briefly taking a leave of absence in the fall of 1864 to campaign for Lincoln's re-election. After the war, he returned to politics, serving in both the House and the Senate. Logan was active in veterans' affairs and is credited with being the man who successfully promoted Memorial Day. John Logan died in Washington, D.C. on December 26, 1886.

COMMANDING
THIRD DIVISION
SEVENTEENTH ARMY CORPS

MAJOR GENERAL
JOHN A. LOGAN

ILLINOIS

The Shirley House

"The Confederates, knowing that they must soon retreat behind their fortifications at Vicksburg, began their preparations by destroying what they could outside, and burned all the houses in the vicinity; but my mother's persistent refusal to go out of hers, and her determination to prevent its destruction, delayed its being set on fire until the Federals made their appearance on the hills to the east of us. The poor fellow who was appointed to do the work, while holding the ball of blazing cotton to the corner of the house, was struck by a bullet of the pursuing vanguard, and crept away under the shelter of some planks, where he died alone. His body was found the next day and buried under the corner of the house."

Alice Shirley,
Vicksburg Civilian
Quoted in Alice Shirley and the Story of Wexford Lodge edited by Terrence Winschel p.20.

Alice Shirley was a 19-year-old Union sympathizer who lived with her parents at Wexford Lodge, a big white house situated in the quiet fields outside Vicksburg. The Shirleys owned about 25 slaves, whom the younger Shirleys addressed as "aunt" and "uncle." The family was ostracized by their neighbors because of their outspoken Union allegiance. When the Union army came to surround Vicksburg, the Confederate troops ordered all civilians outside the city to evacuate their homes and take refuge inside the city itself, while they burned the houses to leave them useless for the advancing Union army. Only Alice's mother and the family slaves were at home when the Confederate troops came to evict her and burn her home. She refused to move.   When the Yankees came, she had a difficult time convincing them of her Union sympathies. However, she eventually succeeded and they allowed her to stay in the house, which unfortunately, they had already ransacked. During the siege, she had her field hands dig a cave into the side of the hill near their home and moved there to avoid the constant shelling and bullets.

Illinois Memorial

"At 4:30 o'clock the mine was sprung, and before the dirt and smoke cleared away, the Forty-fifth Illinois had filled the gap made by the explosion and were pouring deadly volleys into the enemy. As soon as possible, loop-hole timber was placed upon the works for the sharpshooters, but the enemy opened a piece of artillery at very close range on that point, and the splintering timbers killed and wounded more men than did the balls, and I ordered the timbers to be removed. Hand-grenades were then freely used by the enemy, which made sad havoc amongst my men, for, being in the crater of the exploded mine, the sides of which were covered by the men, scarcely a grenade was thrown without doing damage, and in most instances horribly mangling those they happen to strike."

Brig. Gen. Mortimer D. Leggett, USA
Commanding First Brigade, Third Division, 17th Army Corps
Quoted in Guide to the Vicksburg Campaign, edited by Leonard Fullenkamp, Stephen Bowman & Jay Luvaas, p. 427

The Illinois Memorial stands near the Third Louisiana Redan, the scene of desperate assaults by Union forces. The charge on June 25, 1863, after the explosion of a buried 2,200 pound mine, was led by the 45th Illinois Volunteer Infantry. This magnificent memorial pays tribute to the Illinois soldiers that participated in the Vicksburg Campaign. The memorial itself is topped by a golden eagle, representing the nation once again reunited in peace. The relief under the eagle portrays the Muse of History, flanked by figures of women symbolic of the North and the South, each telling her their respective stories. There are 47 steps leading up to the portico at the entrance to the memorial.   The steps symbolize the 47 days of siege endured by soldiers and civilians alike. Inside the memorial are 60 bronze tablets listing the names of every native son who participated in the campaign. The memorial itself cost over $195,000, which was 20% of the state's budget.

Logan's Approach

"Here we are still in the rear of the Rebel Stronghold and still at work Bombarding both by day and Night. We still keep advancing on there Works our Rifle pits are up almost close to there Forts now and I think there will be another trial of there Forts in a few days. Genl Logan has undermined one of there Forts and put in a large quantity of Powder to try to blow it up but it did not do them much damage but he is still at work and is going to give them another trial and I hope will meet with better Success."

Private Thomas Townsend, USA
23[d] Wisconsin Volunteer Infantry
Quoted in Sacrifice at Vicksburg: Letters from the Front edited by Susan T. Puck, p. 65

Union Major General John A. Logan commanded the Third Division of Major General James B. McPherson's 17th Army Corps. During the siege, his engineers dug a sap, or trench, toward the Third Louisiana Redan. The saps were not a straight line toward the Confederate defenses. Rather, they were a series of zig zag trenches designed to give the Union sappers some protection against Confederate fire. The trenches were interconnected to allow movement between the forces.   Any available soldier was enlisted to dig the trenches. After digging for a month, Logan's approach was used to set off the mine underneath the Third Louisiana Redan. Although the redan was entered, it could not be held. Logan set about digging another tunnel under the Confederate defenses and exploded a second mine a week later.

Third Louisiana Redan

"At the appointed moment it appeared as though the whole fort and connecting outworks commenced an outward movement, gradually breaking into fragments and growing less bulky in appearance, until it looked like an immense fountain of finely pulverized earth, mingled with flashes of fire and clouds of smoke, through which could occasionally be caught glimpses of some dark objects – men, gun carriages, shelters etc."

Captain Andrew Hickenlooper, USA
Chief Engineer, 17th Army Corps
Quoted in The Vicksburg Campaign: April, 1862-July, 1863 by David Martin, p. 154

On May 22, 1863, Union forces assaulted this position, which was a major Confederate stronghold along the Jackson Road. The attack failed, and Union General Ulysses S. Grant devised a new strategy: blow up the redan. For weeks, Union engineers dug an approach trench (sap) toward the Confederate fortifications and eventually burrowed a forty-foot tunnel underneath the walls of the redan. Union sappers packed 2,200 pounds of black powder into the tunnel. On June 25, 1863, the mine was exploded and troops from the 45th Illinois charged into the redan supported by 150 cannon. The Confederates had not been fooled, and had moved into a position on higher ground farther back. Despite entering the redan, Union forces could not hold it against the fierce Rebel fire, and retreated the next day. On July 1st, the Yankees tried again, exploding another mine, but having learned from the first assault, did not try another infantry charge. It was not necessary, as Vicksburg was surrendered three days later.

Old Abe and the Wisconsin Memorial

"When the battle commenced, he would spring up and spread his wings, uttering his startling scream, heard, felt, and gloried in by all the soldiers. The fiercer and louder the storm, the fiercer, louder and wilder were his screams."

Captain Charles H. Henry, USA
8th Wisconsin Volunteer Infantry
Quoted in The History of Old Abe, The War Eagle compiled by E.B. Heimstreet

As if he had just alighted atop the granite pillar, Old Abe, the mascot of Company C of the 8th Wisconsin Volunteer Infantry, towers over the majestic Wisconsin State Memorial. Captured from the woods of Wisconsin at only a few months old, Old Abe was presented to the unit by a local Eau Claire civilian. Carried on a specially made perch to the left of the regimental colors, the bird attracted the enemy's attention. During the battle of Corinth, Confederate General Sterling Price told his men: "That bird must be captured or killed at all hazards. I would rather get that eagle than capture a whole brigade or a dozen battle flags." Despite being such a target, Old Abe survived the war and returned home to Wisconsin. The state would give this winged icon as a gift to another unit which had its roots in the area. The legendary "Screaming Eagles" of the 101st Airborne wear Old Abe on their patches to this day. On the plaques at the base of the Wisconsin Memorial are the names of all the sons of the state who participated in the Vicksburg Campaign.

WISCONSIN

COLONEL LYMAN M. WARD
LIEUT. COLONEL JAMES W. POLLEYS
MAJOR ASA WORDEN

ENGAGED SKIRMISH, MAY 19;
ASSAULT, MAY 22 SIEGE, MAY 23-JULY 4.
AGGREGATE CASUALTIES 104.
KILLED 18, WOUNDED 55, MISSING 4.
LIEUT. COLIN MILLER MORTALLY
WOUNDED.

2D BRIG. 6TH DIV. 17TH CORPS.

West Virginia Monument

"What was the poor mother doing now, of whom he whispered to me? How little she knew that the eyes that were so dear, now were looking their last on the light! Far away from home and friends, among strangers, the soul was swiftly passing out into the great sea of eternity, the bright hopes of which so softly regulate this life-tide of ours! – passing out – passing out, with a lingering look of unfathomable speech, into my face; for my face told him what my lips faltered in doing."

Mary Webster Loughborough
Vicksburg Civilian
Quoted in My Cave Life in Vicksburg with Letters of Trial and Travel by Mary Webster Loughborough p.171.

The West Virginia Monument represents the one regiment which served at Vicksburg: the 4th West Virginia Volunteer Infantry of Sherman's 15th Corps. The monument is topped by the bust of Major Arza M. Goodspeed, who was killed in Sherman's May 19th assault on the Stockade Redan.

Ewing's Approach

"Every man in the investing line became an army engineer day and night. The soldiers got so they bored like gophers and beavers, with a spade in one hand and a gun in the other."

Unknown Veteran, USA
Quoted in Vicksburg is the Key: The Struggle for the Mississippi River by William L. Shea & Terrence J. Winschel, p. 156

After the failed assaults of May 19th & 22[d], the Union troops settled in for a long siege of the Vicksburg defenses. Realizing they could not directly assault the Confederate positions, they began to dig their way toward them. Pictured is a fine example of the Union approach toward the Stockade Redan. Union approach trenches (saps) were typically dug in a zig-zag pattern, seven feet deep and wide enough for four men to walk abreast. In front of the trench was a sap-roller, usually a large bundle of cane packed with hay or straw which was rolled along as the sap was being dug to absorb the Confederate bullets being fired at the digging men. Parallel trenches were dug between the lines as well in order to better effect communication. Confederate troops would spend the nights repairing their fortifications and burrowing trenches between their lines. Crouched down during the day, on half-rations and digging furiously at night, the misery index for the defenders at Vicksburg was severe.

37th Ohio Monument

"Lieut. A.C. Fisk, aide-de-camp to General Hugh Ewing, was conspicuous in his efforts to encourage and animate them to go forward to the assistance of their gallant comrades, who could be seen already upon the very entrenchments of the enemy, and Sergt. Maj. Louis Sebastian, thirty-seventh Ohio Volunteer Infantry, went along the whole line of the regiment, exposing himself to the heaviest fire of the enemy, exhorting and remonstrating with the men and urging them forward…"

Major General Francis P. Blair, Jr., USA
Commanding Second Division, 5th Army Corps
Quoted in Guide to the Vicksburg Campaign, edited by Leonard Fullenkamp, Stephen Bowman & Jay Luvaas, p. 432- 433

There were 39 Ohio units to participate in the siege at Vicksburg; and there are 39 monuments at Vicksburg National Military Park dedicated to them. The 37th Ohio was part of the May 22[d] Union assault on the Stockade Redan. The Ohioans were sent in immediately following the "forlorn hope" which was the first unit to attack the redan. The "forlorn hope" was a select group of volunteers, typically required to be single and childless due to the high casualties expected among them. The troops massed along the Graveyard Road, but were beaten back by the Confederate defenders. The 37th Ohio was urged forward by Sergeant Major Sebastian, but refused to enter the hail of bullets awaiting them. The 47th Ohio and 4th West Virginia continued the assault, moving around them, but to no avail. The assault on the Stockade Redan was beaten back.

Kansas Monument

"But the war between the states was a very bloody and a very costly war. One side or the other had to yield principles they deemed dearer than life before it could be brought to an end…It is a significant and gratifying fact that Confederates should have joined heartily in this spontaneous move. I hope the good feeling inaugurated may continue to the end."

Major General Ulysses S. Grant, USA
Commander, United States Army of the Tennessee
Quoted in The Personal Memoirs of Ulysses S. Grant, p. 666

An elegant symbol of a restored nation, the Kansas monument rises from a summer field. The circle at the base of the monument represents the United States before the war, the broken circle at its center speaks of the nation torn asunder during the Civil War, and the restored circle at its top represents the country once again at peace after the war. Perched atop the monument is a stylized version of the nation's symbol, a bald eagle. The monument was erected at Vicksburg National Military Park in June 1960.

35

African American Monument

"This charge was resisted by the negro portion of the enemy's force with considerable obstinacy, while the white or true Yankee portion ran like whipped curs almost as soon as the charge was ordered."

Brigadier General Henry McCulloch, CSA
Commander, McCulloch's Brigade
Quoted in Vicksburg: Fall of the Confederate Gibraltar by Terrence J. Winschel, p. 109

The moon rises over the struggling figures atop the African American Monument. Remarkably, the only African-Americans who actually served during the siege at Vicksburg were Confederate. Used mostly as laborers, cooks and teamsters, they were a little acknowledged part of the Rebel army. After the fall of New Orleans, the Union recruited large numbers of troops from among the freed black population and designated them as Native Guards, who were, in the late summer of 1863, redesignated Corps D'Afrique.

Rhode Island Monument

"On the 14th General Parke arrived with two divisions of Burnside's corps, and was immediately dispatched to Haines' Bluff. These latter troops – Herron's and Parke's – were the reinforcements already spoken of sent by Halleck in anticipation of their being needed. They arrived none too soon."

Major General Ulysses S. Grant, USA
Commander, United States Army of the Tennessee
Quoted in The Personal Memoirs of Ulysses S. Grant, p.321

Standing firm atop the granite pedestal, the valiant Rhode Islander waves his tattered battle flag as if to urge his men onward in the fight. Only one Rhode Island regiment served at Vicksburg, the 7th Rhode Island Volunteer Infantry, Second Division of Major General John G. Parke's 9th Army Corps.   The 7th Rhode Island, along with the rest of Parke's 9th Corps, joined Major General Ulysses S. Grant's Army of the Tennessee from the Department of the Ohio during the second week of June 1863. The noose around the neck of the Confederate defenses was being tightened with their arrival.

New Hampshire Monument

"The boom, boom of the mortar fleet every two minutes, the splash of the water against the sides of the boat and the shrill saw-file notes of the myriads of insects on the shores kept one's eyes and ears open, so that sleep was impossible. The writer, with some others, sat on the bow of the boat till a late hour watching the shells as they fell on Vicksburg. We timed the shells as they left the mortars on their aerial flight and found that it took about 18 seconds for them to land in the city."

Captain Lyman Jackson, USA
6th New Hampshire Volunteer Infantry
Quoted in Vicksburg: 47 Days of Siege by A.A. Hoehling, p. 149

The Granite State was represented by the 6th, 9th & 11th New Hampshire Volunteer Infantry Regiments during the Vicksburg Campaign. They were part of Major General John A. Parke's 9th Army Corps, which was dispatched to Vicksburg in the second week of June to shore up Grant's siege operations. The New Hampshire regiments came down the Mississippi and before landing and taking their place on the Exterior Line, amused themselves by watching the destruction of the city.

Pennsylvania Memorial

"The excessive heat, the malaria that settles like a pall of death around the camps upon the Yazoo River, the scarcity of water and its bad quality and the forced marches told fearfully upon all…the hardships which all were obliged to endure were excessive. Water, which the horses refused to drink, the men were obliged to use in making coffee. Fevers, congestive chills and other diseases attacked the troops. Many sank down upon the roadside and died from sunstroke and sheer exhaustion."

Captain Lewis Crater, USA
Adjutant, 50th Pennsylvania Volunteer Infantry
Quoted in Vicksburg: 47 Days of Siege by A.A. Hoehling, p161-162

There were five units from Pennsylvania serving in the siege operations at Vicksburg: the 45th, 50th, 51st, 100th Volunteer Infantry Regiments, and Battery D, Pennsylvania Light Artillery. The commanders of those five units are pictured in graphic relief on the Pennsylvania Memorial. The Pennsylvanians were part of Major General John G. Parke's 9th Corps. The corps was brought down from Kentucky to strengthen Grant's siege lines around Vicksburg. Unused to the steamy Southern weather, the soldiers found the trip to be an arduous one in the torturous Mississippi heat.

HERE BROTHERS FOUGHT FOR THEIR
PRINCIPLES HERE HEROES DIED FOR
THEIR COUNTRY AND A UNITED PEOPLE
WILL FOREVER CHERISH THE PRECIOUS
LEGACY OF THEIR NOBLE MANHOOD

CURTIN   HARTRANFT   LEASURE   DURELL

PENNSYLVANIA

General Grant's Headquarters

"Until this moment I never thought your expedition a success; I never could see the end clearly till now. But this is a campaign; this is a success if we never take the town."

Major General William Tecumseh Sherman, USA
Commander, 15th Army Corps
Quoted in Vicksburg is the Key: The Struggle for the Mississippi River by William L. Shea & Terrence J. Winschel, p. 143

When Union forces began to clear the Mississippi River of the Confederate threat, Brigadier General U.S. Grant was ready to prove his worth. After initial victories at Forts Henry & Donelson, he attracted national attention and his nom-de-guerre, "Unconditional Surrender" Grant. But the costly battle at Shiloh nearly sidetracked his ambitions. Grant regrouped and kept at the Confederates, setting his sights on Vicksburg. For five months he tried every way he could think of to capture the Hill City, but failed. He struck upon the tactic of crossing the Mississippi and attacking the city from behind, winning battles at Port Gibson, Raymond, Jackson, Champion Hill, and the Big Black. After initial assaults on the Vicksburg defenses failed, Grant settled down to besiege the city and starve the Rebel army out. On July 4, 1863, he succeeded. The Vicksburg Campaign solidified his reputation and he went on to take command of all Union forces and received the Confederate surrender of the Army of Northern Virginia at Appomattox Court House on April 9, 1865.

Thayer's Approach

"This approach commenced near the crest of a ridge, ran down the slope which was toward the enemy, and then up the opposite slope of the ravine, toward the ridge on which the salient approach was situated. As it was difficult to defile this approach, blinding was resorted to. Fascines made of cane were used; these, being placed across the trench, which was about six feet deep, formed a roof which hid the movements of our men, and, where well constructed, was impenetrable to musket balls…This approach was sharply resisted by the enemy, who came outside of their line and had to be driven from the ground."

Captains Frederick E. Prime and Cyrus B. Comstock, USA
Chief Engineers of the Army of the Tennessee
Quoted in Guide to the Vicksburg Campaign edited by Leonard Fullenkamp, Stephen Bowman & Jay Luvaas, p. 320

Thayer's Approach looks much as it did before the siege. Confederate troops cut down the trees and gathered the underbrush to build barriers against any Federal assault. Union sappers got all the way to the top of the ridge, but could not take the Confederate position. Because of heavy fire from the Confederates on the hill, Union troops dug a tunnel underneath the present day road behind the approach in order to tote supplies in and out under cover. The tunnel is there today; however, in the early developmental years of the park, The War Department bricked the walls to prevent it caving in.

U.S.
THAYER'S APPROACH.
THE TRENCH FOR THAYER'S APPROACH
TO THE CONFEDERATE WORK IN HIS FRONT
WAS STARTED ABOUT MAY 30,1863,ON THE
NORTH SIDE OF THIS RIDGE,THROUGH WHICH
IT WAS CARRIED BY A TUNNEL PRESERVED
BY THE BRICK ARCH. THE TRENCH ACROSS
THE RAVINE TO THE FOOT OF THE SPUR
SOUTH OF THIS MARKER ABOUT 6 FEET
WIDE AND 6 FEET DEEP WAS COVERED BY
A BLINDING OF BUNDLES OF CANE LAID A-
CROSS IT AND AFFORDING PROTECTION A-
GAINST RIFLE BALLS. THE CONFEDERATES
DID NOT USE ARTILLERY AGAINST THIS
BLINDING. WHEN THE TRENCH REACHED
COVER AT BASE OF SPUR TWO LINES OF
APPROACH WERE STARTED AND THESE LINES
UNITED ON TOP OF THE SPUR TO FORM ONE
APPROACH.

U.S. Navy Monument Memorial

"Mississippians don't know, and refuse to learn... how to surrender to an enemy. If Commander Farragut or Brigadier General Butler can teach them, let them come and try."

Lt. Colonel James L. Autry, CSA
Quoted in Vicksburg is the Key: The Struggle for the Mississippi River by William L. Shea & Terrence J. Winschel, p. 16

Rising 202 feet into a brilliant blue sky, the U.S. Navy Memorial is the tallest monument at Vicksburg National Military Park. At the base are statues of four U.S. Navy fleet commanders. (Farragut, Porter, Davis, and Foote) On May 18, 1862, Flag Officer David G. Farragut, having steamed up the Mississippi River from New Orleans, landed at Vicksburg and demanded the city's surrender. The city refused. The Union Navy then began a bombardment of the city which was to last until Vicksburg finally did surrender more than a year later. The city became a deathtrap as a result of the shelling. The citizens of the town began to dig caves in the surrounding hills for protection. No food could get into the city from the river, and when the Union army closed off access to the outside world, Vicksburg began to starve.

49

Battery Selfridge

"Five 8-inch, four 9-inch, two 42-pounder rifled guns and four 32-pounder shell guns were landed at different points during the siege at the request of the officers commanding divisions, or of General Grant, and whenever officers and men could be spared from the fleet they were sent on shore to man the guns…"

Admiral David Dixon Porter, USN
Quoted in Guide to the Vicksburg Campaign edited by Leonard Fullenkamp, Stephen Bowman & Jay Luvaas, p. 336

The majestic Naval Monument towers above the location of Battery Selfridge as the bust of Lt. Commander Selfridge looks out from the shadows. As the Union forces tightened their hold on Vicksburg, General Grant decided he needed bigger guns to bring the city to heel. He asked Admiral David Dixon Porter for some of his massive naval cannon to be trained onto the Confederate defenses. Porter obliged and designated some of his officers and men to man them. Here at Battery Selfridge, a contingent of naval guns were placed, commanded by Lt. Commander Thomas O. Selfridge, Jr., captain of the USS Cairo when it was sunk by Confederate mines in the Yazoo River on December 12, 1862.

USS Cairo

"Just as we were training on the battery, (2 ½ miles distant) we were struck by a torpedo, which exploded under our starboard bow, a few feet from the center and some 35 or 40 feet from the bow proper just under our provision store room, which crushed in the bottom of the boat so that the water rushed in like the roar of Niagara. In 5 minutes the forward part of the Hold was full of water and the forward part of the gundeck was flooded."

First Class Boy George R. Yost, USN
USS Cairo
Quoted in Hardluck Ironclad: The Sinking & Salvage of the Cairo by Edwin C. Bearss p.99.

The imposing wreck of the U.S.S. Cairo still looks menacing, more than a century after its sinking. On December 12, 1862, the U.S.S. Cairo was steaming up the Yazoo River toward Vicksburg when she encountered a pair of Confederate torpedoes, or mines. These mines were five gallon glass demijohns filled with gunpowder which were attached to a float that held them near the surface of the water. When the U.S.S. Cairo steamed out into the channel and moved ahead, two torpedoes exploded. The Cairo sank to the bottom of the Yazoo River where it remained until its location was discovered in 1956 by Edwin C. Bearss, Warren Grabau, and Don Jacks. The remains of the boat were raised in 1964 and in 1977 the Cairo was brought to Vicksburg National Military Park where she was restored on site. The gaping hole made by a Confederate mine is visible in the lower right-hand portion of the photograph.

National Cemetery

"The game of life was played on a great scale. Men lived and died with locomotive speed. The rattling of musketry, the crash of artillery and the thunder of continuous trains of army wagons, miles in length, made fit music for this war-life and pressed men forward without time or wish to look at 'things behind.'"

Mrs. A.H. Hoge
Philadelphia Sanitary Commission
Quoted in Vicksburg: 47 Days of Siege by A.A. Hoehling, p. 110

Shadows fall on the national cemetery at Vicksburg. The cemetery was established in 1866, long after the fall of Vicksburg and a year after the war had ended. The 17,000 Union soldiers and sailors buried there were difficult to identify by that time. As a result, some 13,000 of the graves are simply marked "unknown." The Confederate dead of Vicksburg are buried in Cedar Hill Cemetery, in Vicksburg.

Fort Hill

"I have just come from Sky Parlor where we went to see another gunboat fight, five boats from below and one terrible monster from above engaged our batteries. In a very short time, we perceived that the monster was disabled and a tug from above came to her relief. Some later, men seemed to leave her side. Then she drifted over to the Mississippi shore and then arose the glad shout 'She is sinking.' Sinking indeed she was and there she lies under water except her chimneys and her horn! ...I don't think any of them will be so anxious to try our batteries again."

Emma Balfour
Vicksburg Civilian
Quoted in Vicksburg, A City Under Siege: The Diary of Emma Balfour, May 16, 1863 - June 2,1863

During the siege, it was not only the troops surrounding the town that the Confederates needed to worry about. On the Mississippi River, the Union Navy was constantly shelling the town, attempting to force it into submission. On May 27, 1863, Confederate guns firing from positions near the river, including this one at Fort Hill, sank the USS Cincinnati, much to the delight of the civilian onlookers. The boat was raised in August 1863, and placed back into service.

C.S.
JOHNSTON'S COMPANY,
TENNESSEE HEAVY ARTILLERY,
RIVER BATTERIES, ARMY OF VICKSBURG.
CAPT. T. N. JOHNSTON.

A DETACHMENT OF THE COMPANY SERVED ONE 3-
INCH RIFLE IN THIS POSITION, FORT HILL FROM MAY 19
TO THE END OF THE DEFENSE, JULY 4, 1863.

Chickasaw Bayou

"My poor brigade!"

Colonel John F. DeCourcy, USA
Brigade Commander, 15th Corps
Quoted in Vicksburg is the Key: The Struggle for the Mississippi River by William L. Shea & Terrence J. Winschel, p. 53

In the distance, past the horseshoe bend of the Yazoo River diversion Canal, lies part of the ground where the bloody battle of Chicasaw Bayou was fought. In late December 1862, General William Tecumseh Sherman steamed his troops up the Yazoo River north of Vicksburg. Landing on December 26, 1862, Sherman intended to rush his troops toward the unoccupied Walnut Hills and take the high ground before the Confederates could get there to defend it. Unfortunately, at the base of the hills was Chickasaw Bayou, a tangled fetid swamp. In order to take the position, the Federals had to slog through the swamp toward a high bluff, which was now occupied by alerted Confederate troops. By the time Sherman launched his frontal assault on December 29th, the Confederates had reinforced their guard to about six thousand troops on the bluff. Sherman's troops numbered more than five times that of the Confederates, but they were below the Rebels in the swamp. The Confederates decimated the Federal troops who were forced to retreat back through the swamp in a pouring rain. The assault had been a complete disaster for the Union troops.

Graveyard Road

"On they come! Our cannon pours forth the deadly, . . . [canister] into their ranks – They fill up the vacant gaps without pausing a moment – They come now in startling proximity to our works – Not a musket yet has been fired by our men – They have received orders to wait until they can see the whites of their eyes – Not a single head is seen above the works, except now and then a solitary sentinel who stands ready to give the fatal signal – They come now within seventy yards of the our lines – Now a thousand heads are above the earthworks – A thousand deadly guns are aimed and the whole lines are lighted up with a continuous flash of firearms and even the hill seems to be a burning smoking volcano. The enemy's solid columns reel and totter before this galling fire – like grass before the mowing scythe they fall. For awhile they pause and tremble before this deadly storm of death and then in confusion and dismay they fall back."

William Lovelace Foster, CSA
Chaplain, 35th Mississippi Infantry
Quoted in Vicksburg: The Campaign That Opened the Mississippi by Michael B. Ballard, pp. 329-330

At 2 o'clock on the afternoon of May 19, 1863, the signal was given to assault the Stockade Redan. The troops charged up the Graveyard Road to the Redan under a hail of vicious fire. The troops braved the fight and reached the redan, but were pinned down by the heavy Confederate fire. During the afternoon, as the men suffered under the sweltering Mississippi sun, ammunition began to run out and the troops were desperate for more. A young musician with the 55th Illinois heard their cries and was one of four men to volunteer to run back for more. Three members of the group were killed outright, but the fourth, 14-year-old Orion P. Howe, though wounded, made it back to Sherman's command post to ask for more ammunition. Fresh boxes of cartridges were rushed forward, but to no avail. The assault on Stockade Redan failed. Orion P. Howe, for his gallant efforts that day, became the youngest soldier to receive the Medal of Honor at Vicksburg.

Stockade Redan

"As they came down the hill one could see them plunging headlong to the front, and as they rushed up the slope to our works they invariably fell backwards, as the death shot greeted them. They came into the very jaws of death and died. Surely no more desperate courage than this could be displayed by mortal men."

Captain James H. Jones, CSA
38th Mississippi Infantry
Quoted in Vicksburg and the War by Gordon A. Cotton and Jeff T. Giambrone, p.74

On May 19th, Major General Ulysses S. Grant tried to storm the Vicksburg defenses. Waiting and ready were members of the 13th U.S. Infantry, one of two regular army units with Grant at Vicksburg. Led by the grand-nephew of George Washington, Captain Edward Washington, the 13th U.S. Infantry leapt into the fight when the signal was given and charged up the right of the Graveyard Road toward the Stockade Redan. Braving a torrent of gunfire, the 13th U.S. Infantry managed to plant their colors on an exterior wall of the Redan. They began digging their bayonets into the walls, trying to gain a foothold to over run the position. The troops were not numerous enough to breach the wall, and remained pinned down on the outside of the Redan, with the Confederates above pouring murderous fire down upon them. Seventeen flag bearers were killed or wounded and the battle flag returned from the fight with 55 bullet-holes in it. For their bravery, Sherman directed that "First at Vicksburg" be emblazoned on their battle flag. The descendant regiment in today's army, the 1st, 2^d & 3^d battalions of the 13th Infantry, conduct basic training at Fort Jackson, SC, and proudly wear "First at Vicksburg" upon their shoulder patches.

Missouri Memorial

"Nobly did the officers and soldiers of this brigade greet every assault…with defiant shouts and a deliberately aimed fire, and hurled them back in disorder. The enemy gained the ditch around the redan to the right of the stockade and occupied it for some time. Colonel Gause of the Third Missouri Infantry, procured some fuse-shell, and, using them as hand-grenades, threw them into the ditch, where they exploded, killing and wounding some 22 of the enemy."

Colonel Francis M. Cockrell, CSA
Commander, First Brigade, Bowen's Division
Quoted in Guide to the Vicksburg Campaign edited by Leonard Fullenkamp, Stephen Bowman & Jay Luvaas, p. 436

Standing proudly, her arm raised in triumph, the Spirit of the Republic graces the front of the Missouri Memorial. The state sent units to both sides of the conflict and that fact is reflected in its dedication to Missouri's Union and Confederate sons. Inside the Stockade Redan, the defending troops were some of General Pemberton's best. The men of Bowen's Division had fought at Port Gibson, Champion Hill, and Big Black, but were not demoralized by those defeats. The Stockade Redan was braced for an attack, the forest surrounding the position having been cut down to make abatis, (trees and branches cut into spikes and plunged into the ground as obstacles meant to break up Union formations). While the Union forces assaulted the Stockade Redan on the 19th and 22^d of May, 1863, the Confederate defenses held. Siege operations were commenced against the redan, with saps being dug toward it. The position remained, however, in Confederate hands until the surrender on July 4, 1863.

Arkansas Memorial

"On this day, about 2 P.M., the enemy, preparatory to a charge, moved his whole force as near our lines as could be done, and then made a most desperate and protracted effort to carry our lines by assault. This assault was preceded by a most furious fire from the enemy's numerous batteries, of shell, grape, and canister. The air was burdened with hissing missiles of death."

Colonel Francis M. Cockrell, CSA
Commander, First Brigade, Bowen's Division
Quoted in Guide to the Vicksburg Campaign edited by Leonard Fullenkamp, Stephen Bowman & Jay Luvaas, p. 436

Arkansas troops were part of Bowen's Division, some of the most experienced and fiercest fighters in Pemberton's Army. They were positioned inside the Stockade Redan, warding off vicious assaults from Major General Francis Blair's 2[d] Division of Sherman's 15th Corps. The Arkansas Memorial holds aloft the sword of a divided nation. At its base is the altar of faith where that divided nation is reconciled. On the left side of the monument, Arkansas' soldier sons charge in battle; on the right, the CSS Arkansas steams toward the defense of Vicksburg.

ARKANSAS

TO THE ARKANSAS
CONFEDERATE SOLDIERS
AND SAILORS A PART OF
A NATION DIVIDED BY
THE SWORD AND REUNITED
AT THE ALTAR OF FAITH

Surrender Interview Site

"In the afternoon, the division to which I belonged marched in and took formal possession. In our regiment was a boy who had a brother in the Rebel Army in Vicksburg. As we came to their works, the brother was there to meet the boy in our regiment. Our boy fell out of ranks, and they walked together, arms around each other's waists. It was a sight most impressive and one to remain vivid a life time – the one in blue with uniform fresh, buttons shining, gun and bayonet bright; the other in gray, ragged uniform, barefoot and grimy. It was enough to make one feel sad that such things had to be."

Captain Joel W. Strong, USA
10th Missouri Volunteer Infantry
Quoted in Vicksburg & the War by Gordon A. Cotton and Jeff T. Giambrone, p. 94

On July 1, 1863, General John C. Pemberton sent a circular to his generals advising them that the situation at Vicksburg had become untenable and asking them if their troops would be able to evacuate the city, carrying their own supplies and ammunition as there were no longer draft animals to do the task. The generals agreed that their troops had suffered enough and that an evacuation was impossible. By this time Pemberton had also received a letter signed "Many Soldiers," advising him that if he could not feed his troops, he should surrender them rather than have the men of his army disgrace themselves by desertion. Pemberton had no choice. He could not break the siege without help from Johnston, who was not coming. He could not break out. He had to surrender. On July 3, 1863, he sent a letter under flag of truce to General Grant, asking for terms. U.S. Grant, as his nom-de-guerre implied, told Pemberton he wanted unconditional surrender. The next day, July 4th, after an evening of negotiations through an exchange of notes, terms were agreed upon and the surrender ceremony was held at 10 A.M. The Confederate troops marched out, stacked their arms, and returned to their camps to await parole. With the defeat of the Army of Northern Virginia at Gettysburg, PA the day before, the tide of the war had turned.

SITE OF
INTERVIEW BETWEEN
MAJGEN U.S. GRANT
U.S.A.
AND
LTGEN PEMBERTON
JULY 4TH 1863

The Great Redoubt

"The Seventh Missouri and Seventeenth Illinois carried the ladders, forty in number and twelve feet long. The cannon were throwing a heavy fire into the fort and kept it up until our columns moved over the brow of the hill, when the cannon nearly ceased firing, and as our columns moved over the hill in plain view of the enemy, . . . [the Rebels] raised in their forts and poured a heavy volley into our ranks and many of our boys were wounded and killed. Our orders were not to fire till we got into their works, and as we moved up in front of the mouth of the cannon and a volley of musketry and were not allowed to fire, it seemed like madness. There we had to lay under a galling fire until the Seventh Missouri and 81st Illinois were mowed down and found it was foolish to remain longer."

Diarist Charles E. Smith of the 32d Ohio
Quoted in: Volume III, The Vicksburg Campaign: Unvexed to the Sea by Edwin C. Bearss, p. 822

The Great Redoubt was the main Confederate fortification along the Jackson Road. On May 22, 1863, three days after Sherman's initial assault on the Stockade Redan to the north, the Union troops attacked all along the Confederate defenses, including this imposing fortress. The Yankees were driven back, however, as the Rebels poured intense fire into their ranks. As the Union troops came up toward the Redoubt, the Confederates would roll lighted cannonballs down the hill toward the approaching soldiers, which proved devastating to the men. The Union soldiers were forced to withdraw and spent the balance of the siege digging approach trenches toward the Confederate defenses, continually shelling its inhabitants.

Tilghman Monument

"During this time, Tilghman, who had been left with his brigade upon the other road, almost immediately after our parting, met a terrible assault of the enemy, and when we rejoined him was carrying on a deadly and most gallant fight. With less than 1,400 effective men he was attacked by from 6,000 to 8,000 of the enemy with a fine park of artillery; but being advantageously posted, he not only held them in check, but repulsed him on several occasions, and thus kept open the only line of retreat left to the army. The bold stand of this brigade…saved a large portion of the army…"

Major General William W. Loring, CSA
Commander, Loring's Division
Quoted in Guide to the Vicksburg Campaign edited by Leonard Fullenkamp, Stephen Bowman & Jay Luvaas, p. 262

Brigadier General Lloyd Tilghman was a brigade commander in Loring's division. On May 16, 1863, at the battle of Champion Hill, Tilghman was ordered to hold his position near the Raymond Road crossing of Baker's Creek at all costs. As the main portion of Pemberton's Confederates retreated across Baker's Creek toward the Big Black, Tilghman encouraged his men to hold the line to give their compatriots time to escape. As he was personally manning an artillery piece, he was struck by shrapnel and killed. His men were cut off from the main Confederate body heading toward the Big Black River and slipped off with the rest of Loring's Division to join General Johnston's forces in and around Jackson.

BRIGADIER GENERAL LLOYD TILGHMAN C S A
COMMANDING FIRST BRIGADE OF LORING'S DIVISION
KILLED MAY 16 1863
NEAR THE CLOSE OF THE BATTLE OF CHAMPIONS HILL MISS

Mississippi Memorial

"None but those who have had the experience can tell the feeling of the soldier's heart on the night before the approaching battle – when upon the wings of fond imagination his soul visits the loved ones at home – and while he thinks of a lonely & loving wife whose face he may never look upon again & who may never see his form any more on earth, his heart bleeds & dark forebodings fill his mind. Then when he lies down upon the cold ground & looks up to the shining stars above, the gloomy thought crosses his mind, that it may be the last time he will ever look upon the shining heavens & that those same stars which now look down so quiet upon him, may behold him on the morrow night a lifeless, mangled corpse."

William Lovelace Foster, CSA
Chaplain, 35th Mississippi Infantry
Quoted in Vicksburg: Fall of the Confederate Gibraltar by Terrence J. Winschel, p. 85

The Mississippi Memorial was almost not a part of Vicksburg National Military Park. Still distressed from the defeat of its troops at Vicksburg, the host state was unenthusiastic about putting any memorial on federal property. After much vigorous debate, the state legislature agreed to appropriate the funds for the memorial.   The obelisk was dedicated in 1909. The bronze work was placed on the memorial in 1912.

Pemberton Monument

"I now heard everyone speaking of the fall of Vicksburg as very possible, and its jeopardy was laid at the door of General Pemberton, for whom no language could be too strong. He was freely called a coward and a traitor. He has the misfortune to be a Northerner by birth, which was against him in the opinion of all here."

Lieutenant Colonel James Fremantle
Her Majesty's Coldstream Guards
Quoted in The Fremantle Diary: A Journal of the Confederacy, p. 92

John C. Pemberton was born in Philadelphia, Pennsylvania, in 1814. He graduated from West Point in 1837 and was promoted for bravery in the Mexican War. When the Civil War broke out in 1861, Pemberton, whose wife was Virginia-born, went south to fight for the Confederacy. Almost immediately, he was under suspicion because of his birth. Pemberton became a favorite of Jefferson Davis, however, and progressed rapidly through the ranks. Despite General Joseph E. Johnston's refusal to come to his aid, Pemberton was accused of surrendering Vicksburg too soon. After the war, Pemberton was a pariah in the South, having been blamed by Johnston of causing the Confederate disaster by disobeying his orders. Pemberton retired to a farm in Warrenton, Virginia. He eventually moved back to Pennsylvania. He died in Penllyn, PA in 1881 and is buried in Laurel Hill Cemetery in Philadelphia, PA.

Jefferson Davis Monument

"I hope that our separation may be peaceful. But whether it be so or not, I am ready, as I have always been, to redeem my pledge to you and the South, by shedding every drop of my blood in your cause."

Jefferson Davis, CSA
President, Confederate States of America
Quoted in Vicksburg and the War by Gordon A. Cotton and Jeff T. Giambrone, p.9

Jefferson Davis was considered a son of Vicksburg. Born in Kentucky in 1808, he graduated West Point in 1828 and fought in the Black Hawk War, at one point having charge of the captive chief, Black Hawk.   He was at Brierfield near Vicksburg when he was told he had been voted President of the Confederate States of America, a position he did not want, but accepted reluctantly. When General Robert E. Lee's army surrendered on April 9, 1865, Davis had already fled from Richmond and the White House of the Confederacy. The Confederate government met for the last time on May 5, 1865, in Washington, GA and officially dissolved the institution. Davis was arrested on May 10th, stripped of his citizenship and held as a prisoner for two years at Fort Monroe, VA. Upon his release he traveled, became president of the Carolina Life Insurance Co., and wrote two books on the history of the Confederacy. Jefferson Davis died in 1889 at the age of 81.

Texas Memorial

"This is the fourtieth day we have lain in these ditches with the enemys deadly Missels passing in showers over our heads and their Deadly canon battering away at our works and about one hundred of our Regt have been killed and wounded and still no success is at hand yet. I think we can not hold as but few more days more…Rations getting very slim curtailed to 2 ½ biscuit and a Slice of Meat per day I think the siege of Vicksburg has very near played out."

Private Alex Frazier, CSA
2^d Texas Infantry
Quoted in Vicksburg: Southern Stories of the Siege by Gordon A. Cotton

Defiantly standing amongst the palmetto fronds, a Texas soldier remains ready to defend his position. The Texas Memorial stands at the point where Waul's Texas Legion drove the Union troops from the Railroad Redoubt. The Redoubt had been built to defend the approach to Vicksburg along the Southern Railroad of Mississippi. During the assault of May 22, 1863, the Union troops, having blasted an opening in the Redoubt by a vicious artillery barrage, sent men from the 22^d Iowa pouring into the Redoubt. The soldiers of Waul's Texas Legion jumped into the breach and in fierce hand to hand combat beat the Yankees back. One member of the initial assault force of 12 men, Sergeant Joseph E. Griffith of the 22^d Iowa, survived the charge, but he brought back nearly a dozen prisoners with him.

Railroad Redoubt

"Suddenly the roar of the guns ceased…I sprang to my feet and looked in the direction of the enemy, when they seemed to be springing from the bowels of the earth a long line of indigo a magnificent line in each direction, and they kept for a while the alignment as on dress parade, but moving at the double quick…It was a grand and appalling sight."

Lt. J.M. Pearson, CSA
30th Alabama Infantry
Quoted in Vicksburg is the Key: The Struggle for the Mississippi River by William L. Shea & Terrence J. Winschel, p.150

It was here at midmorning of May 22, 1863, that Union troops managed to force their way into the Confederate defenses. Soldiers from Illinois and Iowa poured into the ditch in front of the redoubt and crawled up the walls, forcing the Confederates to retreat and taking Lieutenant Pearson and a dozen of his fellow Rebels captive; yet the Yankees were unable to hold the position. The Confederates sent up reinforcements and drove the Federals out of and back from the redoubt.

Stephen D. Lee Monument

"By this time there was great confusion, the slaughter dreadful. Gen. Lee repeatedly rallied his men – appealed to them by all their love of home and country to rally, threatened to shoot the first who ran, but all to no purpose. Just then he sent Lieut. Underhill to order up ammunition and as soon as he left he was cut off from his General, but could see him, the last man on the field, trying to rally the fleeing men and the bullet falling in a shower around him. One horse had been killed under him (his large bay). He had mounted another. When Lieut. Underhill looked – or as soon as he could see – he looked and he was not to be seen, so he thought he must have fallen immediately. He wept as he related all this, and said he never saw such daring, such generalship, but alas it was all of no avail. He said he was not ashamed of his tears, for God had never made a purer, braver or nobler man."

Emma Balfour
Vicksburg Civilian
Quoted in Vicksburg, A City Under Siege: The Diary of Emma Balfour, May 16, 1863 - June 2,1863

Stephen D. Lee was the youngest lieutenant general in the Confederate army. He served with distinction throughout the war.   After the war, he became the president of the Agriculture & Mechanical College of Mississippi (now Mississippi State University) and devoted much of his time to veterans' affairs. He worked to preserve the land around Vicksburg and was the first chairman of the Vicksburg National Military Park Commission. He died in Vicksburg on May 28, 1908, after welcoming veterans of four regiments of Iowa and Wisconsin soldiers to a reunion, 45 years after fighting them upon the same ground.

Alabama Memorial

"The work was constructed in such a manner that this ditch was commanded by no part of the line, and the only means by which they could be dislodged was to retake the angle by a desperate charge, and either kill or compel the surrender of the whole party by the use of hand-grenades. A call for volunteers for this purpose was made and promptly responded to by Lieut. Col. E.W. Pettus, Twentieth Alabama Regiment, and about 40 men of Waul's Texas Legion. A more gallant feat than this charge has not illustrated our arms during the war."

Major General Carter L. Stevenson, CSA
Commander, Stevenson's Division
Quoted in Guide to the Vicksburg Campaign edited by Leonard Fullenkamp, Stephen Bowman & Jay Luvaas, p. 410

The Alabama Memorial is placed on the spot where troops from Brigadier General Stephen D. Lee's Third Brigade of Stevenson's Division fought. On May 22, 1863, the Alabamians were defending the lines at the Railroad Redoubt when men from the 22^d Iowa managed to capture a portion of the redoubt. Colonel Pettus of the 20th Alabama and men of Waul's Texas Legion retook the position. The fighting all along the Confederate lines was desperate and resulted in an estimated 3,100 Union casualties. After a few days, the dead had begun to decompose in the Mississippi heat and the wounded were suffering in agony. The Confederates were complaining that the Yankees were trying to "stink us out of Vicksburg." On May 25th, General Pemberton sent a message to General Grant under the flag of truce suggesting a cessation of hostilities for a few hours in order to bury the dead and care for the wounded. This proposal was agreed to by General Grant and during the next few hours men of both armies intermixed, conversing pleasantly, sometimes playing cards or singing while their compatriots dug graves for the dead and brought the wounded off the field.

Georgia Monument

Inscription on the Georgia Monument

The Georgia Monument is dedicated those Georgians who gave their lives during the Vicksburg Campaign. The monument is identical to those placed at Gettysburg and Antietam. Georgia troops, under the command of Brigadier General Seth M. Barton (First Brigade, Stevenson's Division) and Brigadier General Alfred Cumming (Second Brigade, Stevenson's Division) saw savage fighting at Champion Hill. After that serious defeat, the brigades retreated to the defense of Vicksburg. Though their position did not see as much fighting as others along the Vicksburg defenses, the Georgians were subjected to constant shelling and sniper fire as well as the privations of siege life: starvation and disease.

Fort Garrott

"At about 1 P.M. a heavy force moved out to the assault, making a gallant charge. They were allowed to approach unmolested to within a good musket range, when every available gun was opened upon them with grape and canister, and the men, rising in the trenches, poured into their ranks volley after volley with so deadly an effect that, leaving the ground literally covered in some places with their dead and wounded, they precipitately retreated."

Major General Carter L. Stevenson, CSA
Commander, Stevenson's Division
Quoted in Guide to the Vicksburg Campaign edited by Leonard Fullenkamp, Stephen Bowman & Jay Luvaas, p. 409

Although Fort Garrott is at the southernmost point of Vicksburg National Military Park, it was not the end of the Confederate defenses surrounding Vicksburg. The Confederate line stretched around the city to the Mississippi. Fort Garrott, or Square Fort as it was sometimes called, was named after Colonel Isham W. Garrott of the 20th Alabama who was killed by a Union sharpshooter near this position. Union Brigadier General Alvin Hovey, whose troops arrived on May 24th, after the initial assaults on May 19th & 22d, attempted to capture this fort by digging trenches, or saps, toward it. The fort was bombarded regularly from Union guns and the Confederates responded in kind, killing men daily as they dug their approaches toward the fort. Union sappers got within 50 feet of Fort Garrott before the surrender of Vicksburg on July 4, 1863.

Indiana Monument

"We move on, and amid all the din and confusion, and rising high above the roar of the battle, can be heard the voices of the brave boys of the 69th Indiana singing, 'We'll rally round the flag, boys.'"

Private M.A. Sweetman, USA
114th Ohio Volunteer Infantry
Quoted in Vicksburg: The Campaign That Opened the Mississippi by Michael B. Ballard, p. 343

Dappled sunlight falls on the figure of Oliver Perry Morton, governor of Indiana during the Civil War. The state was home to one of the most colorful characters of the Vicksburg siege. Second Lieutenant Henry "Coonskin" Foster of the 23^d Indiana Volunteer Infantry. Coonskin, so named for the cap he wore despite the brutal Mississippi heat, was a veteran Union sharpshooter. He would sneak toward the Confederate defenses during the night and dig himself deep into the ground, leaving only a peep-hole from which he would shoot the Rebels. Coonskin built a tower from rails taken from the local railroad, thick enough to be bullet-proof. The structure soon towered over the Confederate defenses near the Third Louisiana Redan, enabling Coonskin and his fellow sharpshooters to kill individual unsuspecting Confederates lying in their trenches. "Coonskin's Tower", as it was called, stood for the duration of the siege despite the many Rebel attempts to blast it down. During the siege it became a popular attraction for Union troops rotated off the line. Coonskin began charging twenty-five cents for admission to his tower, a sizable amount in 1863. One person he did not charge, however, was General Grant, who took to visiting the tower often to examine the Confederate lines. Upon one occasion, the general leaned too far out of the tower and was advised by an observant Confederate, in rather salty language, to get his head down or get it shot off.

Iowa Memorial

"Reaching them, the width and depth of the ditch in front of the works combined with the heavy fire poured into them by the rebels, checked the main advance of the Twenty-second and Twenty-first Iowa. A few brave men, however, leaping into the ditch, clambered up the sides of the fort, rushed into it, engaging in hand -to-hand conflict with the rebels occupying the outer wing of the fort, overcame them, killing many and compelling the remainder to surrender. Thus a portion of their works were in our position, with the flag of the Twenty-second Iowa planted upon the walls."

Brigadier General Michael K. Lawler, USA
Commander, Second Brigade, 14th Division, 13th Corps
Quoted in Guide to the Vicksburg Campaign edited by Leonard Fullenkamp, Stephen Bowman & Jay Luvaas, p. 406

After a vicious four hour artillery barrage, troops of McClernand's 13th Corps poured into the ditch at the front of the Railroad Redoubt. Clawing their way up the walls of the redoubt, Sergeant Joseph E. Griffith of the 22[d] Iowa and a dozen men breached the wall where the artillery had pounded it down and in ferocious hand-to-hand combat, managed to force the Rebels to retreat. Of the original dozen assailants, only a few, including Griffith, managed to survive the assault. Forced back by troops from Waul's Texas Legion and the 30th Alabama, Griffith escaped the redoubt, bringing a dozen prisoners out with him. The Yankees could not exploit their success in gaining a portion of the redoubt and were forced to withdraw. The Vicksburg defenses held.

McClernand Monument

"I have found it necessary to relieve Major-General McClernand, particularly at this time, for his publication of a congratulatory address calculated to create dissension and ill-feeling in the army. I should have relieved him long since for general unfitness for his position."

Major General Ulysses S. Grant
Commander, United States Army of the Tennessee
Quoted in Guide to the Vicksburg Campaign edited by Leonard Fullenkamp, Stephen Bowman & Jay Luvaas, pp. 309-310

Although he disliked abolitionists, McClernand was fierce in his support of the Union. When the war broke out, he discovered a talent for raising money and troops. Lincoln appointed him Brigadier General of U.S. Volunteers in August of 1861. In February 1862, McClernand took command of a division in the Army of the Tennessee. He was reassigned in October to raise a new army to move against Vicksburg. He sent his Army of the Mississippi to Memphis, where it was commandeered by William T. Sherman who nearly destroyed it in his failed assault against Chickasaw Bayou. McClernand assumed personal command and led it in a successful assault against Arkansas Post in January 1863. It was then absorbed into the Army of the Tennesse as the 13th Corps, with McClernand in command. During the assault on Vicksburg, McClernand's troops were the only ones to briefly take possession of a portion of the Confederate defenses, but were unable to hold them.

The Widow Blakely

"On the 22nd, at 9 A.M., four iron-clads and one wooden gun-boat engaged the lower batteries, and after an engagement of one hour and a half were repulsed. Two of the iron-clads were seriously damaged. This engagement was creditable to the First Louisiana Artillery, who, with ten guns, mostly of smaller caliber, contested successfully against thirty-two heavy guns of the enemy. Our casualties were only 2 wounded during the fight; one 10-inch Columbiad and the 18-pounder rifled gun were temporarily disabled. The Blakely gun burst at the muzzle."

Colonel Edward Higgins, CSA
Commander, River Batteries
Quoted in Guide to the Vicksburg Campaign edited by Leonard Fullenkamp, Stephen Bowman & Jay Luvaas, pp. 452

The Widow Blakely is a 7.5-inch rifle designed by British Captain Theophilus Alexander Blakely. It was nicknamed "The Widow" because it was the only gun of that make mounted at Vicksburg. During the siege, a round prematurely exploded in the muzzle. The Confederates trimmed off the damaged parts and used the gun as a mortar for the rest of its service. After the war, the gun was sent to West Point, where it was misidentified as "Whistling Dick," another famous gun of the Vicksburg Siege. The Confederates had claimed to have consigned "Whistling Dick" to a watery grave in the Mississippi. When "the Widow's" true identity was discovered, she was returned to Vicksburg and placed on the bluff overlooking the Mississippi River, about a mile south of her original position.

"THE WIDOW BLAKELY"

Because it was the lone Blakely rifled cannon in all the Vicksburg defenses, the Confederate soldiers called this 7.44-inch gun, "The Widow Blakely." During the siege it was mounted about 1 mile north of its present position. On May 22, 1863, the "Widow" was manned by a detachment of Company H, 1st Louisiana Heavy Artillery, Lt. A. L. Slack, commanding the detail.

In that day's action against Union gunboats, one of the "Widow Blakely's" own shells exploded in its muzzle. Later, the Confederates cut away the damaged end and used the gun as a mortar.

After the war, "The Widow Blakely" spent 96 years on display at the U.S. Military Academy's Trophy Point.

U.S. Department of the Interior
National Park Service

Maryland Monument

"His burial was attended by the colonel and staff, the members of his company and a large number of devoted friends. All were more affected than I remember to have seen on any former occasion. The general wept like a child. It was a strange sight – while shot and shell were falling thick and fast to see strong men used to war and blood and death all around them, bend the humble knee, forget their vengeful passions and by the grave of a soldier shed tears like a woman – but so is war."

Captain William H. Claiborne, CSA
Aide-de-camp to Colonel Alexander W. Reynolds, 4th Brigade, Stevenson's Division
Quoted in Vicksburg: 47 Days of Siege by A.A. Hoehling, p. 231

Maryland was a border state during the War, and sent regiments to both sides of the conflict. At Vicksburg, the state was represented by the 3^d Maryland Battery, CSA, commanded by Captain Ferdinand Osman Claiborne. On June 25th, Captain Claiborne, nicknamed "Ferd," thought he saw the enemy approaching his position. He borrowed a field telescope from his cousin William and ran to his battery to check out the situation. He had barely given the order to fire when he was struck in the face by a shell fragment. He died a few minutes later, his cousin by his side.

MARYLAND

STEVENSON'S DIVISION
THIRD CONFEDERATE BATTERY
CAPTAIN FERD O. CLAIBORNE
CAPTAIN JOHN B. ROWAN

ENGAGED CHAMPION'S HILL MAY 16
DEFENSE, MAY 18—JULY 4. CASUALTIES
NOT FULLY REPORTED CAPTAIN FERD O.
CLAIBORNE KILLED JUNE 24. ON DUTY
AT GUNS IN FRONT OF THIS MONUMENT
A DETACHMENT WITH ONE GUN UNDER
LIEUT. WILLIAM L. RITTER SERVED ON
ROLLING FORK AND DEER CREEK FROM
APRIL SECOND TO JUNE FIRST WHEN IT
WAS ORDERED TO YAZOO CITY AND
ATTACHED TO WALKER'S DIVISION.

North Carolina Monument

"He also said that Johnston's army consisted of the very flower of the South Carolina, Virginia, and Kentucky troops. This was corroborated by a courier, who came in the same day, and reported himself as only three days absent from Johnston's camps. Joseph E. Johnston was our angel of deliverance in those days of siege, but alas! We were never to even touch the hem of his robe."

Lida Lord
Vicksburg Civilian
Quoted in Vicksburg: 47 Days of Siege by A.A. Hoehling, p. 206

North Carolina, South Carolina, Mississippi, and Kentucky troops were an integral part of General Joseph E. Johnston's Confederate Army of Relief. During the campaign leading up to the siege of Vicksburg, Joe Johnston's Army was driven out of Jackson by troops led by Ulysses S. Grant. Johnston considered his army too small to raise the siege of Vicksburg and stayed in and around Jackson for the duration of the siege, despite repeated cries for help from his beleaguered generals trapped inside the starving city. On July 1, Johnston moved his army toward the Big Black River, but unwilling to risk his force, did not attack Grant. Two days later, after Pemberton was forced to surrender Vicksburg, he moved his forces back to Jackson.

NORTH CAROLINA

JOHNSTON'S ARMY
FRENCH'S DIVISION
McNAIR'S BRIGADE
29TH INFANTRY
LT. COL. WM B. CREASMAN
39TH INFANTRY
COL. DAVID COLEMAN
BRECKINRIDGE'S DIV
STOVALL'S BRIGADE
60TH INFANTRY
COL. WASH. M. HARDY
LT. COL. JAS. M. RAY

BY THE STATE
IN HONOR OF
HER SOLDIERS
ENGAGED IN THE
VICKSBURG OPERATIONS

Pemberton Headquarters

"Just thirty years ago I began my military career by receiving my appointment to a cadetship at the U.S. Military Academy, and to-day – that same date – that career is ended in disaster and disgrace."

Lieutenant General John C. Pemberton, CSA
Commander, Confederate States Army of Vicksburg
Quoted in Vicksburg: Fall of the Confederate Gibraltar by Terrence J. Winschel, p. 81

In October 1862, John C. Pemberton took command of the Department of Mississippi and East Louisiana and managed to hold off General U.S. Grant for several months. Things fell apart in the spring, however, when Pemberton began receiving conflicting orders from both President Jefferson Davis and General Joseph E. Johnston who had been sent to Mississippi by Davis to reverse the declining Confederate fortunes there. After Grant crossed the Mississippi, Pemberton was torn between defending Vicksburg at all costs and joining up with Johnston's army to defeat Grant. After Confederate losses to Grant at Port Gibson, Raymond, and Jackson, Pemberton finally moved his army east from Edwards Station to join up with Johnston's army which had been defeated at Jackson, but still tried to keep a tenuous hold on Vicksburg. Pemberton ran into Grant at Champion Hill, however, and suffered a devastating defeat. He changed direction and retreated back toward Vicksburg, losing many men in another vicious battle at Big Black River. Pemberton withdrew into Vicksburg where he endured a 47 day siege before surrendering to Grant on July 4, 1863. Pemberton was right. His career was essentially over.

PEMBERTON
HEADQUARTERS
(Willis-Cowan House)

Built ca. 1835. Military headquarters of Lt. Gen. John C.
Pemberton, who commanded
the Confederate forces during
the siege of Vicksburg. Here
the decision
on July 3, 1863, the decision
was made to surrender the city.

Old Court House

"You may be sure that none of us raised our eyes to see the flag of the enemy…Every house was closed and every house filled with weeping inmates and mourning hearts."

Margaret Lord
Vicksburg Civilian
Quoted in Vicksburg: Southern Stories of the Siege by Gordon A. Cotton

Today the Old Court House is a museum dedicated to Vicksburg/Warren County history. In 1863, however, the court house was the most visible building in the town, located at one of the highest points in the city. During the siege, many civilians would go up to the balcony around the cupola of the courthouse to get a good view of the activity of gunboats on the river, as well as the entrenchments around the city. The Yankees marched to the court house on July 4th after the surrender of Vicksburg and raised the Stars and Stripes over the same cupola where so many civilians had waited and watched, praying for a Confederate victory. The occupation of Vicksburg had begun.

Bibliography

Ballard, Michael B. The Campaign for Vicksburg. Washington, DC: Eastern National, 1996.

Ballard, Michael B. Vicksburg: The Campaign that Opened the Mississippi. Chapel Hill, NC: North Carolina University Press, 2004.

Bearss, Edwin C. Hardluck Ironclad: The Sinking and Salvage of the Cairo. Baton Rouge, LA: Louisiana State University Press, 1966, 1980.

Bearss, Edwin C. The Vicksburg Campaign: Unvexed to the Sea, Vol. III, Morningside Books, Dayton, Ohio, 1991

Botkin, B.A., ed. A Civil War Treasury of Tales, Legends and Folklore. New York: Random House, 1960.

Cotton, Gordon A. Vicksburg: Southern Stories of the Siege. Vicksburg: Gordon A. Cotton, 1988.

Cotton, Gordon A. & Giambrone, Jeff T. Vicksburg and the War. Gretna, LA: Pelican Publishing Co., 2004.

Fullenkamp, Leonard, Bowman, Stephen & Luvaas, Jay, ed. Guide to the Vicksburg Campaign. Lawrence, KS: University Press of Kansas, 1998.

Grant, Ulysses S. The Personal Memoirs of Ulysses S. Grant. New York, Smithmark Publishers, Inc.: 1994.

Heathcoate, T.A. Battles in Focus: Vicksburg. Havertown, PA: Casemate Publishing, 2004.

Hoehling, A.A. Vicksburg: 47 Days of Siege. Mechanicsburg, PA: 1996.

Lord, Walter, ed. The Fremantle Diary: A Journal of the Confederacy. Short Hills, NJ: Burford Books, 1954.

Loughborough, Mary Webster. My Cave Life in Vicksburg. Vicksburg, MS: Vicksburg & Warren County Historical Society, 2003.

Martin, David. The Vicksburg Campaign: April, 1862 – July, 1863. New York, NY: Gallery Books, 1990.

Mullins, Michael A. & Winschel, Terrence J. Vicksburg: A Self Guiding Tour of the Battlefield. Wilmington, NC: Broadfoot Publishing Co., 1990.

Platt, Fletcher, ed. The Civil War in Pictures. Garden City, NY: Garden City Books, 1955.

Puck, Susan T., ed. Sacrifice at Vicksburg: Letters from the Front. Shippensburg, PA: Burd Street Press, 1997.

Richard, Jr., Allan C. & Richard, Mary Margaret Higginbotham. The Defense of Vicksburg: A Louisiana Chronicle. College Station, TX: Texas A&M University Press, 2004.

Shea, William L. & Winschel, Terrence J. Vicksburg is the Key: The Struggle for the Mississippi River. Lincoln, NE: University of Nebraska Press, 2003.

Simpson, Brooks D. Ulysses S. Grant: Triumph Over Adversity 1822-1865. New York: Houghton Mifflin, 2000.

Walker, Peter F. Vicksburg: A People at War 1860-1865.Wilmington, NC: Broadfoot Publishing Co., 1987.

Ward, Geoffrey C., Burns, Ric & Burns, Ken. The Civil War: An Illustrated History. New York: Alfred A. Knopf, Inc., 1990.

Weinberger, Phillip C., ed. Vicksburg, A City Under Siege: Diary of Emma Balfour May 16, 1863 – June 2, 1863. Washington, DC: Eastern National, 1983.

Winschel, Terrence J., ed. Alice Shirley and the Story of Wexford Lodge. Washington, DC: Eastern National, 1993, 2003.

Winschel, Terrence J., ed. The Civil War Diary of a Common Soldier: William Wiley of the 77th Illinois Infantry. Baton Rouge, Louisiana University Press, 2001.

Winschel, Terrence J. Vicksburg: Fall of the Confederate Gibraltar. Abilene, TX: McWhiney Foundation Press, 1999.

VICKSBURG

A PHOTOGRAPHIC JOURNEY
WITH VOICES FROM THE PAST

Published by Artistry in Photography
P.O. Box 491 Langhorne, PA 19047

artistry in photography(TM)

Visit us on line at: www.artistryinphotography.com